The Orphan Trains:

Leaving the Cities Behind

Edited by Jeanne Munn Bracken

*Details of orphans "off to the West"
from* Harpers' *magazine illustration, August 1873.*

Discovery Enterprises, Ltd.
Carlisle, Massachusetts

© Discovery Enterprises, Ltd., Carlisle, MA 1997

ISBN 1-878668-87-0 paperback edition
Library of Congress Catalog Card Number 96-86719

10   9   8   7   6   5   4   3   2   1

Printed in the United States of America

Subject Reference Guide:

Cataloging in Publication Data:

The Orphan Trains: Leaving the Cities Behind
edited by Jeanne Munn Bracken
Perspectives on History Series

Orphan Trains — Juvenile Literature

Orphans — I. Title   II. Series   III. Editor

Dewey 362.7   LC HV 985
Summary:
Stories of some of the orphans "placed out" from Eastern cities,
mostly into the American heartland — who they were,
why they went, and what happened to them.

Acknowledgments:

Materials included in this book are detailed in the bibliography; those collected by the Orphan Train Heritage Society of America have been especially moving and helpful. Special thanks to Mary Ellen Johnson for permission to excerpt those documents. Also, thanks to Mr. and Mrs. Paul Landkamer for their assistance and support.

The assistance of my colleagues at the Lincoln (MA) Public Library and throughout the Minute Man Library System is gratefully recognized. Carolyn Birmingham (interlibrary loan services) and Beverly Shank (Medford Public Library) have also gone beyond the call of duty.

Cover photo: Boys in an alley on Mulberry St., NY, 1889. Jacob A. Riis.

Table of Contents

Dedication

This book is affectionately dedicated to my husband Raymond Ronald Bracken, and in the spirit of the orphan trains, to the siblings of his formerly scattered family, newly reunited after fifty-two years: Ermyle (Wyoming), Merle (Nebraska), and Jerry (Minnesota).

The Orphan Trains

by
Jeanne Munn Bracken

Imagine you are a child of the city. You are used to crowded slums, city streets, being hungry. Maybe you are living on your own, stealing what you need for survival. Your clothes are ragged. You can't read, don't go to school, may be working for a few pennies — selling newspapers, or shining shoes. Maybe you have a parent (or even two), or you may be on your own. You might even be responsible for your brothers and sisters, trying to protect them as you fend for yourselves in dark alleys and warm doorways.

Then you are taken from the streets and put in an orphanage with many other children. You may be separated from your friends and siblings. You are scrubbed up, dressed like all the other children, and you usually get enough to eat. You go to school and worship services. If you long for your former life, it isn't far away — maybe just over the orphanage wall.

Then you are loaded on a train with other children, many of them strangers. You are being "placed out." The train, clacking mile after mile along the rails over mountains, rivers, and prairies, will pull into a station where a swarm of strangers will look you over, feeling your muscles, examining you for illness or weakness. One of them might choose you to go home with him. If you are small in stature, you will have to stand on a box — so the crowd can look you over. You are being "put up for adoption." You might become one of the family — loved, well-fed, educated. *Or maybe nobody will want you!* Then, you will be left alone on the train after all the other children are taken. Where will your journey end?

With all of our modern ideas and laws about adoption, foster care, child labor, and family values, it is difficult to imagine that such a thing could happen to a person. Yet it did, and not all that long ago. Many people are still alive at the end of the twentieth century who were moved from city orphanages to new homes — or forced into unpaid labor as indentured servants — by a system called "Placing Out." Beginning before the Civil War, children from eastern cities were removed from their homes (if indeed they had any homes) and transported to the Midwest, the South, and elsewhere by what are today popularly called the "orphan trains."

Over the course of generations and centuries, social forces, such as urban versus rural populations, change. In the early years of the United States, everybody lived either in a village or on a farm or plantation; but as the country grew, so did the cities. This process accelerated with the Industrial Revolution, when people were drawn to the cities for factory work; in many cases, the cities grew up around the factories.

With that growth came new problems. Housing was often poor, factory work could be dangerous, and large families were difficult to support in the cities. The mid-nineteenth century was also a period of immigration to the United States — and a period of westward movement of many Americans into the lands beyond the Mississippi. Life was precarious. A worker's slight slip, an illness, a wagon accident, childbirth — any of these incidents, and many more, could destroy a family by killing or disabling the wage earners. In the towns and countryside, neighbors would pick up the slack, helping out until the family was stabilized.

In the cities, however, neighborliness was less likely to save people in distress. City neighbors were not known for helpfulness, and the government in those days was not set up to handle social problems like orphaned (or unsupervised) children. Charities (especially religious organizations) bore the burden of caring for those unable to care for themselves. In 1850, in New York City alone, among a population of 500,000, there were an estimated 30,000 children living on the streets.

In 1853, Reverend Charles Loring Brace founded the Children's Aid Society to help these children. First he gathered boys and girls from the streets and placed them in orphanages in and around the city: places with names like the New York Juvenile Asylum, Randall's Island Orphanage, the American Female Guardian Society and Home for the Friendless, and, in Boston, the New England Home for Little Wanderers. Those who were old enough to learn a trade were sent to places like the Brace Farm School for vocational training. Soon others like the Sisters of Charity of Saint Vincent de Paul followed Brace's lead. But the children's homes couldn't handle all of the waifs who needed help. A more permanent solution was required.

Charles Loring Brace

Brace was something of a visionary. He thought there must be people of good will in the countryside who would welcome another child into their homes. He believed there were small businesses where youths, like apprentices, could learn a trade and provide assistance while they were learning. Brace put his theory to work. Beginning in 1854, trains clattered from the East with carloads of unusual freight: children for the American heartland.

"Placing out" worked and the experiment continued. During the peak year, 1875, 4,026 children were "sent out." In the year Charles Loring Brace died, 1890, another 2,851 children were moved. Even in the post-World War I era, the orphan trains streamed west, carrying children orphaned by the war or by the terrible influenza epidemic that followed closely on its heels.

Not everyone praised the system. Some thought the children were being sold into slavery. Others were afraid that the city institutions were just moving a social problem out of their own neighborhood and into someone else's, sending what would today be called juvenile delinquents out to the prairie. Virtually all of those who made the journey were white children of European ancestry; sickly or retarded children were left behind. The system didn't work very well with children over twelve.

Although regular church attendance was stressed as a criterion for receiving one of the children, most of the early adopting families were Protestants, to which Catholics objected. The latter responded by creating the New York Foundling Hospital, which pre-selected farm families and assigned foundling infants to them before the "baby trains" left the cities.

In their zeal to find places for the children, the local committees sometimes didn't screen the homes as well as they could have. Some children were certainly abused physically and mentally. Some were clearly not well treated, whether from malice or more benign causes.

In 1929, the last train rolled from New York City to Missouri. The final tally of orphan train riders is in dispute; surely there were more than 100,000 of them, and most historians now accept the toll as 200,000. These children and youth found homes in forty-seven states and territories from Florida to Texas, as well as in Canada and even Europe.

Fortunately, through the efforts of organizations like the Orphan Train Heritage Society of America, these children are no longer forgotten. Their remarkable stories, gathered in several collections, speak for themselves — sad, funny, angry, touching — in short, the entire human experience.

In the following text, excerpts from the children's letters and journals, along with some of their reminiscences as adults, are presented. In some cases, children and grandchildren of the orphans recount stories of their family members who rode the orphan trains to a new life.

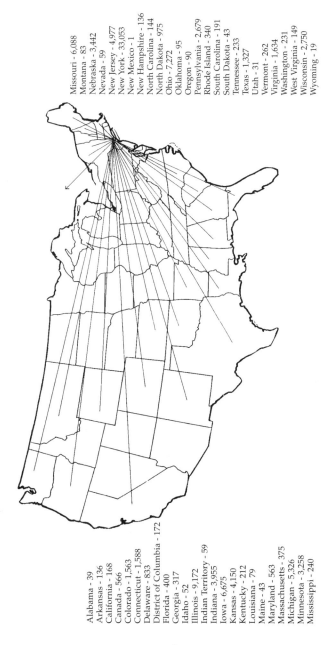

Alabama - 39
Arkansas - 136
California - 168
Canada - 566
Colorado - 1,563
Connecticut - 1,588
Delaware - 833
District of Columbia - 172
Florida - 400
Georgia - 317
Idaho - 52
Illinois - 9,172
Indian Territory - 59
Indiana - 3,955
Iowa - 6,675
Kansas - 4,150
Kentucky - 212
Louisiana - 79
Maine - 43
Maryland - 563
Massachusetts - 375
Michigan - 5,326
Minnesota - 3,258
Mississippi - 240

Missouri - 6,088
Montana - 83
Nebraska - 3,442
Nevada - 59
New Jersey - 4,977
New York - 33,053
New Mexico - 1
New Hampshire - 136
North Carolina - 144
North Dakota - 975
Ohio - 7,272
Oklahoma - 95
Oregon - 90
Pennsylvania - 2,679
Rhode Island - 340
South Carolina - 191
South Dakota - 43
Tennessee - 233
Texas - 1,327
Utah - 31
Vermont - 262
Virginia - 1,634
Washington - 231
West Virginia - 149
Wisconsin - 2,750
Wyoming - 19

By 1910, 47 states, Canada, District of Columbia and the Indian Territory had taken children from the Orphan Trains under the care and oversight of the New York Children's Aid Society. (Map from Orphan Train Heritage Society)

The Problem of the Children

Source: Jacob A. Riis, *How the Other Half Lives; Studies Among the Tenements of New York* 1890; reprint edition, Cambridge, MA: Belknap Press of Harvard University Press, edited by Sam Bass Warner Jr., 1970.

"I counted the other day the little ones, up to ten years or so, in a tenement...the house contained 170 children [in 40 families]....I tried to count the children that swarmed [in an alley] but could not. Sometimes I have doubted that anybody knows just how many there are about. Bodies of drowned children turn up in the rivers right along in summer whom nobody seems to know anything about. When last spring some workmen, while moving a pile of lumber on a North River pier, found under the last plank the body of a little lad crushed to death, no one had missed the boy, though his parents afterward turned up. [In one tenement] of 478 tenants...only seven [children admitted] they went to school. The rest gathered all the instruction they received running for beer for their elders. Some of them...slept in the streets at night.

Sleeping on Mulberry St., New York. Photo by Jacob A. Riis

The official came upon a little party of four drinking beer out of the cover of a milk can in the hallway. They were of the seven good boys and proved their claim to the title by offering him some....

A little fellow who seemed clad in but a single rag was among the flotsam and jetsam stranded at Police Headquarters one day last summer. No one knew where he came from or where he belonged. The boy himself knew as little about it as anybody, and was the least anxious to have light shed on the subject after he had spent a night in the matron's nursery. The discovery that beds were provided for boys to sleep in there, and that he could have a 'whole egg' and three slices of bread for breakfast put him on the best of terms with the world in general, and he decided that Headquarters was a 'bully place'.

...[He was asked] 'Where do you go to church, my boy?'

'We don't have no clothes to go to church.' And indeed his appearance, as he was, in the door of any New York church would have caused a sensation.

'Well, where do you go to school, then?'

'I don't go to school,' with a snort of contempt.

'Where do you buy your bread?'

'We don't buy no bread; we buy beer,' said the boy, and it was eventually the saloon that led the police as a landmark to his 'home.' It was worthy of the boy. As he had said, his only bed was a heap of dirty straw on the floor, his daily diet a crust in the morning, nothing else.

...Whence this army of homeless boys?...The answer is supplied by the procession of mothers that go out and in at Police Headquarters the year round, inquiring for missing boys, often not until they have been gone for weeks and months, and then sometimes rather as a matter of decent form than from any real interest in the lad's fate. The...promise of the clerks who fail to find his name on the books among the arrests, that he 'will come back when he gets hungry,' does not always come true. More likely he went away because he was hungry. Some are orphans, actually or in effect, thrown upon the world when their parents [went to jail]....Grinding poverty and hard work beyond the [lad's ability]; blows and curses for breakfast, dinner, and supper; all these are recruiting agents for the homeless army. Sickness in the house, too many mouths to feed."

Ragamuffins by Jacob A. Riis

"Don't live nowhere!"

Source: Charles Loring Brace, quoted in Leslie Wheeler's "The Orphan Trains," *American History Illustrated*, vol. 18, 1983, pp. 10-23.

"Most touching of all was the crowd of wandering little ones who immediately found their way to the [Children's Aid Society] office. Ragged young girls who had nowhere to lay their heads; children driven from drunkards' homes; orphans who slept where they could find a box or stairway; boys cast out by stepmothers or stepfathers; newsboys, whose incessant answer to our question 'Where do you live?' rung in our ears, 'Don't live nowhere!' Little bootblacks, young peddlars, 'canawl-boys,' who seem to drift into the city every winter, and live a vagabond life; pickpockets and petty thieves trying to get honest work; child beggars and flower sellers growing up to enter courses of crime — all this motley throng of infantile misery and childish guilt passed through our doors, telling their simple stories of suffering, and loneliness, and temptation, until our hearts became sick; and the present writer, certainly, if he had not been able to stir up the fortunate classes to aid in assuaging these fearful miseries, would have abandoned the post in discouragement and disgust."

The Orphanages

William Paul Landkamer

Source: William Paul Landkamer, from Mary Ellen Johnson and Kay B. Hall, eds., *Orphan Train Riders: Their Own Stories*, Gateway Press, Baltimore: 1992.)

"As I remember the foundling Hospital, it was a large brick building with a black iron fence all around a large bare yard with no trees, there were both small and large children there. The home was located in the metropolitan area of the city, we could stand and look through the bars of the fence and watch the traffic and people go by on the street. I recall one day all of us kids were standing at the fence looking out through the bars, a man passed by and gave me a banana, I did not get one bit of it because an older girl grabbed it out of my hand and ate the whole thing. I never got another banana that I can recall while I was there. The inside of the home had long wide halls, along the walls were large, red, crock jars spaced along either side, these jars were about four feet high and three feet in diameter, I never saw anything protruding out from the top so I do not know what they contained. I now believe they contained water to fight fires, in those days there were no sprinkler systems to fight fires nor any modern equipment as we have today. I remember a large room with lots of small white iron beds, we little kids were put into them by older girls in the home. This is where we slept. There was a smell of cooking at the home that has stayed with me all these years..."

Maude Slyter

Source: Story of Maude Slyter from Johnson and Hall, *op. cit.*

"I was placed in a nice home, and lived in this home till I was nearly ten years old. Ill health of my foster mother compelled these people to return me back to the Kansas Home Society. I stayed in the home for quite awhile. Each child had a chore of some kind to do, to help keep the home up.

I will never forget the big pile of plates, at the table, setting in front of the Matron. She put your helping of food in the plate and passed it to the first child to her left or right, and they had to pass it on; this kept up till we were all served. You had to eat everything in your plate, if you liked it or not, and if you did not eat every bite, it was saved for you for the next meal and would be sitting on the table at your place, no matter what they had good to eat at this meal. You could not have anything else, that was your punishment, so you learned to eat all that was put in your plate and like it, and be glad that you did."

"Mealtime" at the New York Foundling Hospital, about 1900.
(Courtesy of the Museum of the City of New York, The Byron Collection)

Sarah Tjebkes

Source: Sarah Tjebkes, from Johnson and Hall, *op. cit.*

"She stayed for awhile [at an orphanage] and could remember going outside to the toilet. It had a long seat with many holes to use. On stormy days and nights it was very scary."

15

Mamie Rose Gunderson

Source: Mamie Rose Gunderson, from Johnson and Hall, *op. cit.*

"Now I'll describe the orphanage...in Brooklyn, New York. Inscribed in large stone letters on the front of the building as you go up the long, wide steps was 'Industrial Home for Destitute Children.' This orphanage had to be large to house nearly 800 children. It contained a school, chapel, hospital, and wards. The hospitals and wards were on the fifth floor, also dormitories.

The building was divided into two wings. The center was spacious which was a part of the nursery and also school rooms. The first floor was a dining room where both boys and girls ate their meals. The dining room consisted of long, narrow tables like our picnic tables, and we sat on stools. At each place was a granite cup of milk and two slices of bread. This was our meals, three times a day with one exception, on visiting days we had soup.

Also, on this floor, was the girls' playroom. The bathroom was a large tub with water pipes overhead. Also, there was a long trough where each girl would wash her face and hands and scrub her head before going into the dining room each morning. You wonder why I said scrub her head. The girls had their hair cut short with clippers so they could scrub their hair each morning.

...The girls and boys were separated entirely even on the playground. The playground was all cement with a brick wall all around and a brick wall to separate the boys from the girls. No trees or grass so, for a shelter, there was a roof which extended over both the boys' and girls' playground. Also extending all around the playground was a high brick wall. No one could climb in or out....The girls' dormitory was on the fifth floor, also a detention room and hospital. I was in the hospital once when I had the chicken pox. I had the chicken pox so mild. I enjoyed being in the ward as we had nice beds and pillows and play toys.

...In the summertime, we went to the park. Of course, we marched there and stayed together and marched back. Everything we did, we went by the bell and everywhere we went we marched in single file. There was a bell for rising in the morning and a bell to march to the dining room....Everything had to be orderly. We were disciplined so strict. We couldn't do any talking at any time except on the play ground and play rooms....We didn't have many toys. All I remember was a dolls' trunk, which had been donated by the churches.

...The clothes we wore were all alike. The girls wore plaid dresses ...long sleeves, an apron of blue and white check was worn over the dress, so we made one change once a week, a clean apron. The boys wore a dark suit with a checked apron over the suit."

Five Points Nursery, evening prayers. Photo by Jacob A. Riis

The Idea

Source: "The Little Laborers of New York City" in *Harper's New Monthly Magazine*, vol. 47, August 1873, pp. 321-332.

"Another ingenious effort for the benefit of the destitute children of the city is the 'placing out system' which has been carried out by the Children's Aid Society during the last 20 years with such remarkable success. The society early saw the immense benefit in taking advantage of the peculiar economical condition of this country in treating questions of pauperism. They at once recognized the fact, and resolved to make use of their plans, of the endless demand for children's labor in the Western country. The house-keeping life of a Western farmer is somewhat peculiar. The servants of the household must be members of the family, and be treated more or less as equals. It is not convenient nor agreeable for a Western matron to have a rude European peasant at the same table and in the same room with the family. She prefers a child whom she can train up in her own way. A child's labor is needed for a thousand things on a Western farm. Children, too, are valued and thought much of. The same opportunity is given to working children as to all other children. They share fully in the active and inspiring Western life. They are moulded by the social tone around them, and they grow up under the very best circumstances which can surround a poor boy or girl. No treatment which man could devise could possibly be so beneficial to the laboring children of this city as that offered by Western farms. Moreover a child's place at the table in our rural households is of small account. Of food there is enough and an abundance. Generosity, and especially toward children, is the rule in our Western districts. This benevolent association, taking advantage of these great facts, early made arrangements for scattering such little workers of the city as were friendless and homeless all through the Western country. Western agents are employed who travel through remote farming districts, and discover where there is an especial call for children's labor. An arrangement is then made with the leading citizens of the village to receive a little detachment of these homeless children of the great city.

On a given day in New York the ragged and dirty little ones are gathered to a central office from the streets and lanes, from the industrial schools and lodging-houses of the society, are cleaned and dressed, and sent away, under charge of an experienced agent, to 'seek a new home in the West.' When they arrive in the village a great public meeting is held, and a committee of citizens formed to decide on the applications. Farmers come in from 20 to 25 miles round looking for the 'model boy' who shall do the light work of the farm and aid the wife in her endless household labor; childless mothers seek for children that shall replace those that are lost; housekeepers look for girls to train up; mechanics seek for boys for their trades; and kind-hearted men, with comfortable homes and plenty of children, think it is their duty to do something for the orphans who have no fair chance in the great city. Thus in a few hours, the little colony is placed in comfortable homes. Subsequently, if changes should be necessitated, the committee replace the children, or the agent revisits the village, while a steady correspondence is kept up by the central office with the employers. In this way something like 25,000 boys and girls have been placed in country homes during the past 20 years. Nearly 3000 a year are now sent forth by the society. Great numbers of these children have acquired property, or have grown up to positions of influence and respectability."

The Children's Aid Society annual report for 1864 related the following:

"Little N., with three brothers and an elder sister, was brought to our office by her father to get homes for all of them, the mother being a miserable drunken creature, who would pawn and sell everything for rum. N., when we got her (being a little over a year old), was much bruised from the falls she had received while with her mother. The father, a respectable mechanic, fearing that the evil course of the mother would set his children too bad an example, thought it expedient to remove them to Western homes. All the children have excellent homes."

*This New York ad about boys being sent to Kansas for "placing out,"
encouraged New Yorkers to donate to the Children's Aid Society.*

Getting Ready

Clara B. Homestock began with the Children's Aid Society in 1903, and was an agent with them until 1944. The excerpt below was published in the Northwood (Iowa) Anchor *in 1944.*

Source: Patricia J. Young and Frances E. Marks, eds., *Tears on Paper: The History and Life Stories of the Orphan Train Riders,* 1990: Belle Vista, Arkansas.

"(In the beginning) I thought it was the most incredible thing imaginable to expect people to take children they had never seen and to give them a home, but we placed them and never failed to accomplish it....We were constantly attempting the impossible and [achieving it]....

First came the assembling of children in New York. They were gathered up from various places...some came from the Children's Homes and Counties of Western and Northern New York State, some from Institutions in Brooklyn and New York City; and others from the homes of the [Children's Aid] Society; The Brace Farm School and the Girl's Home, now the Goodhue Home on Staten Island. The usual procedure was for an agent to visit the Institution, see the children, and get some idea of their health, mentality and personality....The girls and younger children were outfitted the day before the trip and were given two changes of clothing throughout with a nice silk or wool dress, hat, coat and gloves. The boys were dressed in the basement of the Children's Aid Society, as at present, and were given an outfit similar to that of the girls. Many comments were made on how nicely they were dressed. The thought was that the children must look as well groomed as those of the children in the community where they were to go....The number of children in the parties taken varied, from ten to thirty would be the usual number. Mr. R. N. Brace [son of the founder] thought nothing of taking a party of from 20 to 30 boys to Texas where the local worker had secured homes for most of them before they started from New York. There were local workers in Missouri, Kansas, Nebraska, Iowa and Texas.

The children taken were of all ages, from babies in arms to boys and girls of 16. Brothers and sisters were placed together, or in the same neighborhood so that they saw each other frequently. This policy still continues. At Canton, S.D., we placed a family of seven brothers and sisters....We grew much attached to the children and to the small babies, but understood that the foster parents should come first in the mind of the child. The babies always called forth the most interest and this interest helped to place older children, so that we tried to take a baby with each party.

Artist's version of the inside of a typical day coach in the late 1800s.

The trips were planned so as to arrive on Friday, usually leaving New York Tuesday noon. No one used a Pullman coach, a day coach served us. The children would curl up on the seats at night and sleep sweetly, they made the trip but once. The attendants had at least two days and nights of sleeplessness and four if Texas, West Kansas or Nebraska was the destination. We took a streetcar from the office with the children, their lunch, and the smaller children's bundles. The older children's clothing was carried in the Society trunk. The lunch was put up in 6 or 8 enormous boxes and the agents assisted in doing this. It was carried with us to the train....We were let on the train before the rest of the passengers and had everything in order when they came in. We filled one end of the car or, if the party was large enough, a coach was put on for us. A varied amount of food was carried, loaves of graham and white bread and all sorts of sandwich fillings, ham, cheese, peanut butter, lettuce, celery and mayonnaise dressing, figs, dates and raisins, apples, oranges and bananas, cakes and cookies, and cans of condensed milk for the younger children and babies. Many of the children were carsick, due to the fact that most institution children then were malnutrition cases. Later as children were given a balanced diet, this trouble was rare. Our own homes fed their children well and they were nearly always in good physical condition. Physicians examined them in the homes, but there were no mental clinics.

At the station in New York, the Societies' huge trunk was checked and the emergency bag taken out for the trip. We were always in fear that the clothing of the children might not arrive with us. The emergency bag contained knives, forks and spoons, bibs, towels, washcloths and soap, tooth paste, sewing kit, sterno burner to heat the milk for the babies, blankets and knitted shawls for the babies, medicine for colds and coughs, burns, etc., and larkspur in case any vermin [fleas] should escape the vigilant eye of the caretaker at the different homes. The agents took their personal trunks, as they might be in the west for six months, or might come back in a week. One had to be ready to travel at a minutes [sic] notice.

A change of trains was usually made in either Chicago or St. Louis, and sometimes a change of stations also. If two agents were along this was not hard, for one would go ahead and [the] other follow with the children between, each agent had a baby in her arms, usually and the baggage was distributed among the older children if no porters were available. The older children were always helpful on the train.

The train men...often...gave contributions of money which were sent to the Main Office, but more often gave of candy, chocolate and we were kept busy washing hands and faces. At meal time the rest of the food was apportioned. A drink of milk finished the meal. The children arrived in good condition.

Before the children were sent out they were told about this trip and that they were to receive a real home, with a father and mother, and the kind of homes were described to them. They were made to believe, before leaving New York, that a real home was the nicest possible thing they would have, and so they were happy about going....Then the children in the west would write back telling how happy they were and of the good times they had. They rarely showed any desire to return to New York and soon forgot they had ever lived there."

Boys from the New York Children's Aid Society are photographed before leaving for Texas. (Orphan Train Heritage Society)

En Route

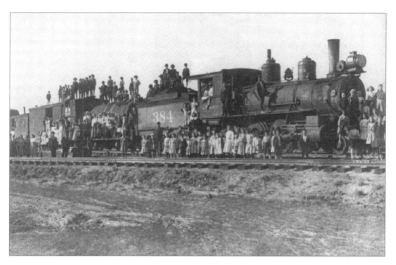

Orphan train riders pose in front of a train on the Achison, Topeka & Santa Fe Railroad line, at the turn-of-the-century. Exact date and location are unknown. (Courtesy of the Kansas State Historical Society.)

The trip west was an eye-opening experience for the children: exciting, yet, frightening. Many of them had never been out of their own neighborhoods, let alone out in the countryside. With few books, no television, no movies, the outside world was unknown to most of the children. Many were leaving behind a parent (and often two) and their entire known world. City streets, slums, perhaps petty theft: these were more familiar than the vast unknown prairies and farms. The first orphan train trip in 1854 carried forty-six boys from New York City (and another who clambered aboard in Albany for the adventure) to Dowagiac, Michigan, changing boats and trains several times. The accompanying agent wrote enthusiastically about the boys' reaction.

Reverend Smith Reports on the Children's Migration

Source: Reverend Smith, from "The Children's Migration," by Annette Riley Fry, *American Heritage*, vol. 26 # 1, December 1974, pp. 4-10.

"...you can hardly imagine [wrote the Reverend Mr. Smith] the delight of the children as they looked, many of them for the first time, upon country scenery. Each one must see everything we passed, find its name, and make his own comments. 'What's that, mister?' 'A cornfield.' 'Oh, yes, them's what makes buckwheaters.' 'Look at them cows (oxen plowing); my mother used to milk cows.' As we whirled through orchards loaded with large, red apples, their enthusiasm rose to the highest pitch. It was difficult to keep them within doors. Arms stretched out, hats swinging, eyes swimming, mouths watering, and all screaming — 'oh! oh! just look at 'em! Mister, be they any sich in Michi*gan*? Then I'm in for *that* place — three cheers for Michi*gan*!' We had been riding in comparative quiet for nearly an hour, when all at once the greatest excitement broke out. We were passing a cornfield spread over with ripe, yellow pumpkins. 'Oh! yonder! look! Just *look* at 'em!' and in an instant the same exclamation was echoed from forty-seven mouths. 'Jist *look* at 'em! What a heap of *mushmillons*!' 'Mister, do they make mushmillons in Michi*gan*?' 'Ah, fellers, *aint* that the country tho' — won't we have nice things to eat?' 'Yes, and won't we *sell* some, too?' 'Hip! hip! boys; three cheers for Michi*gan*!'"

Sarah Tjebkes

Source: Violet Tjebkes Bates, from Johnson and Hall, *op. cit.*, pp. 81-82.

"Sarah [Tjebkes] had a real fascination for trains, and she would go down to the train station and spend hours looking at the trains....When my mother saw a chance to ride a train, she volunteered to take the place of a girl who was sick. She was so happy to go that she couldn't stop laughing, and so she didn't get to have her picture taken with the rest of the group that was going. The thing she remembered most about the trip was wearing long, black stockings and eating large ginger cookies."

Hazelle L. Latimer

Source: Hazelle L. Latimer, from Johnson and Hall, *ibid.,* p. 304.

"...early December, 1918, we boarded the train for Texas. But — before we left I was called to the office. I was told to tell my new family that I was an orphan. I refused. [*Many of the children had living parents; the second largest group, after the orphans, were those who had both living fathers and mothers who were unable or unwilling to care for them.*] I got hit many times with a heavy ruler — palms of my hands. She stopped and asked me if I would say 'no family.' I said no, I would tell the truth, that my Mother was in a hospital and would find me — more whacks — my legs, thighs and up. I still said no — and wouldn't cry. She said, 'Don't you ever cry?' I just looked at her. After one gets so many hits I think I just mentally ruled her out and was numb until the next day. I could not close my hand or sit comfortably.

Now we are aboard the train. It was pretty crowded—two to a seat — in the night. Somewhere in Pennsylvania the conductor came through telling us to all get to one side of the coach as the train would stop and we could all see both ends of the train. The engineer at one end and the brakeman at the other waved to us. We enjoyed that. It was the first time my little Emma laughed. [*Older children were paired with younger ones for the trip; Hazelle was 11 and Emma just 3.*]

Then, the second night was better. The conductor had managed the passengers so that each of us could have a whole seat to stretch out and sleep."

Typical ad for finding homes for children.

28

The Train's Arrival

A typical announcement appeared in the *Jewel County Advocate* serving Mankato (Minnesota):

HOMES FOR ORPHAN CHILDREN

A company of orphan children, under the auspices of the Children's Aid Society of New York, will arrive at Mankato on Friday....These children are from orphanages, both boys and girls two years old and up. They know nothing about street life: well disciplined, well dressed, intelligent children. Parties can take them on trial. Adoption is not demanded. Applicants must be endorsed by a local committee. Those taking children must agree to send them to school the entire school year; also send them to church and Sunday School properly clothed and cared for until they are: boys 17 years old, and girls 18 years.

The following well-known citizens have agreed to act as a local committee to assist the agent in procuring homes: J. P. Fair, B. F. Duncan, N. E. Myerly, A. Temple, S. E. Hill and Robert Gordon.

Distribution will take place Friday...at 10 a.m. at the Mankato opera house.

An address [*speech*] will be given by the agent, J. W. Swan of University Place, Nebraska. Come and see the children and hear the address.

Clara Comstock

"In arrival at our destination, the party went to the hotel where the children were fed, washed and dressed in their best, and if there was time, given a nap. At two o'clock there was a meeting, sometimes called a distribution or reception, of the Committee and the Agents, with anyone interested. These meetings were held in a church, court house, or perhaps in the opera house. While this was going on the children were kept in a group by themselves, and the agent spoke to the people assembled, giving terms of placement and describing the activities of the Society. I have known of [at] least 1500 persons being present. Occasionally there was a mistake in the arrangements, and no one came. This meant arranging for the distribution, and caring for the children while doing it.

The coming of the children to a Community was carefully planned. A town was selected in which no children from our society had been placed by parties for 20 years. This gave a chance for the first ones placed to have grown up. We often came across older boys and girls who were married and doing well, and seldom heard of a failure....

The town selected must have a high grade of citizenship, good schools, and we favored college towns, a fertile and prosperous agricultural community, and be of the same religious faith as the children. Nationality also was considered. In the middle west, whole communities were of German, Danish, Bohemian, Holland, [Norwegian] or Swedish descent. Many of these were superiour, and the children placed with them prospered, but in the main, we preferred the descendents of the settlers from the eastern states. Children were placed in Iowa, Kansas, Missouri and Texas, with occasional parties to North Dakota, South Dakota and Arkansas. We visited children in Colorado and Montana, and other states where foster families had moved. In the earlier days parties were placed in Illinois, Ohio and Indiana, no children were taken over the Rocky Mountains....

The time and place of distribution was announced in the local papers and letters were sent through the rural mails, inviting folks to come to the reception, if interested. The local committee's names were given, and it was made plain that they would take applications before the arrival of the children. Many applications usually awaited us.

After the reception the committee and the agents met, and selected the families who qualified....The family was interviewed and the child selected was sent out with them, with understanding that this was not a placement, but that the agent must come and see the home and talk to the child, before the contract could be signed....It took from one to two weeks to complete the placement of the party."

ASYLUM CHILDREN!

A Company of Children, mostly Boys, from the New York Juvenile Asylum, will arrive in

ROCKFORD, at the Hotel Holland,

THURSDAY MORNING, SEPT. 6, 1888,

And Remain Until Evening. They are from 7 to 15 Years of age.

Homes are wanted for these children with farmers, where they will receive kind treatment and enjoy fair advantages. They have been in the asylum from one to two years, and have received instruction and training preparatory to a term of apprenticeship, and being mostly of respectable parentage, they are desirable children and worthy of good homes.

They may be taken at first upon trial for four weeks, and afterwards, if all parties are satisfied, under indentures,—girls until 18, and boys until 21 years of age.

The indenture provides for four months schooling each year, until the child has advanced through compound interest, and at the expiration of the term of apprenticeship, two new suits of clothes, and the payment to the girls of fifty, and to the boys of one hundred and fifty dollars.

All expenses for transportation will be assumed by the Asylum, and the children will be placed on trial and indentured free of charge.

Those who desire to take children on trial are requested to meet them at the hotel at the time above specified.

E. WRIGHT, Agent.

PLEASE EXTEND THIS INFORMATION.

Ads ran in local newspapers, alerting families to the orphans' arrival.

Charles Loring Brace

Source: Charles Loring Brace, from Fry , *op. cit.*, pp. 4-10.

"The farming community having been duly notified, there was usually a dense crowd of people at the station, awaiting the arrival of the youthful travellers. The sight of the little company of the children of misfortune always touched the hearts of a population naturally generous. They were soon billeted around among the citizens, and the following day a public meeting was called in the church or town hall....The agent then addressed the assembly, stating the benevolent objects of the Society, and something of the history of the children. The sight of their worn faces was a most pathetic enforcement of his arguments. People who were childless came forward to adopt children; others, who had not intended to take any into their families, were induced to apply for them; and many who really wanted the children's labor pressed forward to obtain it."

Guy de Leo

Source: Guy de Leo, from Johnson and Hall, *op. cit.*, p. 287.

"I was born in New York City, April 20, 1913. I remembered a few things at the orphanage, like falling down the long stairway, and eating a lot of prunes, and liking and knowing my nurse, Hanna.

The Orphan Train of about 200 orphans pulled into the St. Paul depot in 1916, and my foster mother met me at the train depot. I was in a long dress, curls down over my shoulders, and a big identification tag was pinned to my dress.

My mother took one look at me, and said to my nurse Hanna, 'I wanted a boy.' Nurse Hanna said, 'If you take a good look you'll find out he is a boy.'

My mother took me to a shop and bought a whole new outfit of boys clothes for me.

The next week in New Ulm, Minnesota was quite hectic. Peop]
to the house to see that boy from the New York Orphanage. I wa
happy about this, but what really got me was: *'Oh, what a beautiful girl!*
From then on, I wanted my mother to cut off my curls."

Hazelle L. Latimer

"Our next stop was the Beckman Hotel, Greenville, Texas. The next
day we went to the Masonic Hall — a traumatic experience for anyone. We were lined up on the stage and all I could see was 'wall to
wall' people. They surrounded us, made us turn around, lift our skirts
to see if our legs were straight, open our mouths to show our teeth, etc.
Very humiliating day. [Three year old] Emma was picked that day.

I went in a buggy with a very old doctor for the night but went back
to the hotel the very next day. I was on the floor, playing....There was
a knock on the open door and I looked up to see the biggest man I had
ever seen. He said he had come for me. I thought — Lord, if he ever
hits me, I'll never recover. It was Mr. Tredway.

We got into his Ford [it was 1918] and out to the country. Mrs.
Tredway met us in the yard, looked into my face. All she said was,
'She is a pretty little thing, isn't she?'

They had a son Hugh, who was 4 years older than me. We all got
along well and the years went by. But, one of the first things I told them
was — 'My mother is not dead.' They went back to Greenville the next
day and Miss Comstock and Miss Hill both said that I was an orphan.

'Dad' did not let that rest. He made several trips to town, talked to
a lawyer — Mr. Vaughan, and finally found out that my mother was
alive, but was in a hospital suffering from a brain tumor and they could
not operate. All they could do was to keep her comfortable as possible. I wrote to her in care of the hospital and got reports about her
until she died in September, 1920."

The following, reprinted in Tears on Paper, *appeared in an otherwise unidentified newspaper called the* Daily Independent, *Friday May 17, 1912:*

BABY DAY
Where and How 56 Babies Found Mothers and Fathers

A sight rarely witnessed, took place at the Union Pacific station yesterday afternoon, when the special coach with babies aboard and with the proper attendants of nurses and sisters [nuns], arrived. Fifty-six of the little ones, two sisters and five nurses, were in the party which occupied one coach as it left New York City, en route to the stretch of country, between Omaha and Grand Island, where these infants were to be given in the care of good people who had arranged to provide for them and make men and women of them. The scene showing the anxious men and women who had 'ordered' a baby and eager to cuddle the little tot in their arms, was in a way, a very touching one and then again, caused no end of merriment. It was 'baby day' at the station, if there is such an event, and a few hundred people witnessed the distribution, and many others would have been willing to have paid a price of admission to have seen it. Some of the women were so anxious to embrace the little ones that they attempted to get into the car, but this was not permitted, and they had to wait their turn, when their baby, properly tagged, was handed out. They were not all the same age, but were in the neighborhood of a year old. Ten were left in Omaha, in Columbus 22, Fremont 2, Schuyler 2, Elkhorn 2; in Grand Island and vicinity 10, in Kearney 6 and two at another point near here.

A representative finds homes for the little tots in advance and the people who were here to receive them, agree to provide a home and take them as their own. Some ordered boys, others girls, some preferred light babies, while others dark, and the orders were filled out properly and every new parent was delighted. They were very healthy tots and as pretty as anyone ever laid eyes on.

These babies were sent from the New York Farming [sic] hospital, a Catholic institution....The babies are trained to go to mothers and fathers and in no case yesterday was there any sign of discomfort shown in not going to the outstretched arms. An old couple, the man wearing a long full beard, was among the recipients and as a baby boy, about a year old, was handed to him, the first baby talk heard was, 'papa.'

Reunited

Source: Quoted in Leslie Wheeler's "The Orphan Trains," *American History Illustrated*, vol. 18, December 1983, pp. 10.

"There were brothers and sisters — four of the party were from one family. As the groups were separated and the smaller ones saw brother or sister taken away by a stranger, the tears flowed. One large boy, whose baby sister was given to a farmer's wife, sat at the edge of the stage and sobbed piteously. But it came out all right. The baby sister, too, cried all night, and the next day the big-hearted farmer drove to town and took the boy. It was difficult to tell which was happier — the farmer or the children."

Herbert Kingsley

Source: Caroline Thompson, from Johnson and Hall, *op. cit.*, p. 57.

"As near as I can ascertain, my father [Herbert Kingsley] was an Orphan Train Rider.

The story, as told to me by my great aunt (who was also my step-grandmother) was that he, along with a group of orphans, was brought in a wagon to Arapahoe or Furnas County around 1890. The children were dispersed to families along the way. My father, who was just a little one, approximately 2 or 3 years old, was left with a Scandinavian family.

My grandfather, who worked for the Sheriff's department, in either Arapahoe City or the County, was out in the country on his way home. He stopped at the Scandinavian's farm and, while there, saw this little dark haired boy among the fair haired children. He inquired and was told that the boy was the smallest of the group of orphans, and the last one left, so the family had taken him rather than have him returned. My grandfather talked them into giving my dad to him.

It was late in the day, and my grandfather was on horseback. Apparently Dad had fallen asleep, so grandfather wrapped him in his coat. When they arrived home, grandfather carried him inside to grandmother, whose birthday it just happened to be. His statement was, 'I brought you a birthday present, Sarah.' From that day on he was their special child, and especially hers. Apparently, they had had one child who died, and could have no more.

My father was one of the fortunate ones who was raised in a loving home. He was 30 years old, shortly after his mother's death, when he found out he was not their natural child. His father refused to discuss it."

A group of children and their agents from the New York Children's Aid Society were photographed upon their arrival in Lebanon, Missouri in 1909.

Settling In

Clara Comstock

"After the party was placed the agent started the annual visiting and this meant continual traveling, sometimes we made as many as 12 trips to New York for children in a year....There were no autos then, a trip behind a livery team meant riding behind a team of mustangs with a driver whose vocabulary consisted of seven words — 'Yes-Mam and No-Mam,' and 'I don't know' and 45 miles was a good days [sic] work. We had a charcoal burner under the robes for our feet, and we sat up in the wind and storm under a top buggy, the thermometer ranging from 36 degrees below zero to 113 degrees above. The mud in Missouri used to be so gummy that the driver carried a knife to cut it away, because it would roll upon the wheel. Sometimes each wheel could weigh a hundred pounds or more. There were few bridges, and if floods came, we forded the streams or stayed where we were. The hotels were very poor, the food inedible. Women were received with suspicion if they traveled alone at night and some hotels refused them admission. In Western Nevada and Kansas, the sand sifted in piles around your closed windows. There was no heat in the bedrooms and the hotel lobby, with its huge stove, was the only place to get warm. In the wild hay country of northern Nebraska, there were no roads, you angled across the prairie. (Once, I was lost 20 miles south of Atkinson, Nebraska, on the prairie on a cold November night....The driver was a one-eyed man and could not see the trail, and I was too much of a tenderfoot to know it.) Any conveyance at all was used to reach the home, lumber wagons, caboose or freight trains, top buggies, sleighs, and later trucks and Fords. "

The following article appeared in the Nebraska Signal *published in Geneva, Nebraska on January 29, 1904.*

'Send Browney Back.'

Source: Reprinted in Young and Marks, *op. cit.,* p. 101.

Plattsmouth, Nebr, Jan 19 — The house of the Rev. J. B. Swan in this city shelters a little brown-haired orphan boy who was brought here from Exeter, Neb., a few days ago. His name is Wilson Vorbew, and although only 7 years of age his short life has been full of pathetic incidents.

While misfortune has been apparent in many ways, yet he is so young and innocent that his consciousness is not burdened with these misfortunes and he seems to be as happy as any other child.

About a year ago "Browney," as the lad is known, was placed in the care of the Children's Aid Society of New York. Soon afterwards a family named Wilson — composed of a husband and wife, living near Exeter — adopted the little orphan. Having no children of their own, the old couple soon held the little fellow as the idol of their hearts, and his sweet presence threw a ray of happiness over the old farm home.

Six weeks ago, however, death entered the Wilson home and removed the foster father. Then, two weeks later death again appeared, taking away the orphan's last and best friend — the foster mother.

The family of J. W. Wolstenholm, who live near the Wilson place, undertook the task of caring for the little fellow until such time as the Children's Home society could find a new home for him. Mr. Wolstenholm's objections to permanently keeping the boy were based upon the fact that his own family was too large — having recently been increased by two other orphan children left by a relative.

The Rev. Mr. Swan, who represents the New York Society in Nebraska, went after little "Browney" last Wednesday. It was at once apparent that the Wolstenholm family had become very fond of the homeless boy, and a pathetic scene preceded the departure of the lad from the home.

Mrs. Wolstenholm, her two grown daughters, and even the head of the home were moved to tears, but Mr. Wolstenholm sternly reiterated his reasons for the stand he had taken in the matter and the other members of the family reluctantly abided by his decision.

Mr. Swan brought the boy to Plattsmouth, intending to bring him upon the pulpit in the Methodist church Sunday morning, and ask that some person open his home to the orphan boy. His plans were changed at the last moment, however, by the receipt of a telegram from the Wolstenholm family, which contained these words: 'Bring "Browney" back.'

Their love for the orphan had prompted them to reconsider and thus it came about that "Browney" will 'go back home.'

Many caring and loving families took the orphans into their homes and loved them as their own.

The societies kept track of the orphans long after they were placed, in an effort to insure that none were mistreated. Not every orphan on the city streets was a candidate for the trains, as Charles Loring Brace agreed: the experiment was less likely to be successful for children over the age of 12 or so. Nor were children sent who had physical or mental handicaps, or children of minority races. Still, Brace bristled at the criticism that he was deporting hooligans to terrorize the midwest as quoted in "The Children's Migration" in American Heritage.

Charles Loring Brace

"We admit, of course, that the large boys change their places, that sometimes a boy is placed in a home where he does not suit the family, or the family him, and in such cases we seek immediately to replace the lad and to make things right in regard to him. We carry on an immense correspondence with the boys and their Western employers; we hear from the committees who are responsible gentlemen of the place, and our own agents are continually travelling through the States where the children are placed. The agents also employ clergymen or other responsible persons in these villages to visit these children."

In fact, one of the weaknesses of the system proved to be the local committees. In small towns and rural areas, it was difficult to turn down an applicant who wished to adopt or employ an orphan. Merchants on the committee were reluctant to offend their customers, and neighbors had to live together afterward. According to later stories told by the orphans, the visiting agents were not always successful in discovering cases of abuse.

Paul Forch

Source: Eileen Berniece Forch Bock, from Johnson and Hall, *op. cit.*, p. 33.

"Paul (Forch) was born, somewhere in New York City, on March 29, 1882, and was orphaned, at three years of age, when he believes his parents were killed in some type of train accident.

He was put into an orphanage in New York City. He thought he vaguely remembered two girls there, who he thought were his sisters, but they were taken out almost immediately, and he did not see them again.

As a young child, he was sent out to Blairsburg, Iowa, on one of the infamous 'Orphan Trains.' He was taken in by a family named Fairchild. He was immediately given tasks too much for such a small child, but he endured. He was not adopted, nor shown one kind act of love. He was treated as a slave; scrubbing wooden floors daily with lye water until his hands bled. His constant diet was potatoes and chicken feet.

As he grew older and grew more bold he learned to steal a piece of fried chicken off the platter when company was expected on Sunday. He knew he would suffer a severe beating after company left, but it was worth it to him.

Years passed by and, as he passed into young manhood, he had learned to hate and not to trust. One day, when he was fourteen years old, he suffered a severe beating. He sneaked out of the house taking his one possession with him (a new pair of boots). He walked down the road several miles to the end of the Fairchild property where he took off his old boots and tossed them back over the fence and put on his new boots. He walked a few miles further to a farm and was given work there. It is not known how long he worked for them, but that opportunity gave him a start in life."

Ethel M. Barney

Source: Robert V. "Bob" Staley, writing of Ethel M. Barney Malone Staley, from Johnson and Hall, *ibid.*, p. 96.

"My mother Ethel M. Barney, age 7 (circa 1903) was taken by Risin and Elizabeth Malone to work on their farm and do housework. Her brother Elmer came to live with them after one year.

Mom gathered eggs, fed the chickens, carried wood and cobs to the house, helped with the washing and housework and worked in the garden. The following summer she milked cows and did other chores. She said she was always busy, but did attend some school nearby. [These chores were probably done by virtually all prairie children in those days — orphan train riders or naturally born.]

She liked her adopted mother, but in later years referred to Risin, her adopted father, as a 'Dirty Old Pup.' When the mother went to town for groceries, she said she would go hide in the woods, barn or fields until Elizabeth returned.

Christmas was always very bleak. Usually an apple or orange, but never a toy or doll. In later years clothes were received. She had but one pair of shoes to wear for school and every day use.

One summer when she was about 12, she went barefooted to save her shoes. When the 4th of July came and the family were going to town to the celebration, her feet had grown and swelled and the shoes wouldn't go on. She had to go barefooted and sat in the wagon all the time. She had not been to town since spring....She did all kinds of chores and once, when chopping kindling, she cut the side of her foot with the axe. They never did take her to a doctor and this foot gave her problems all her life."

A school in Helena, Montana. One of the terms of adoption and indenture was that the orphans had to attend school. (Library of Congress)

Frank Wilson

Source: Rebecca Wilson Richard, writing of Frank Wilson, from Johnson and Hall, *ibid.*, pp. 153-154.

"(Francis Wilson) traveled his road scared, as any 4 year old would be. His Mother, Maggie Wilson, turned her newborn son over with no intention of turning around to see.

Francis, at twelve days old, was baptized at Church Ephiary. His god mother was Mary Burke (who also had another child named Francis.) On the same day she released him.

May 6, 1907 — he made his first of several trips to Opelusas, Louisiana. He was shipped to his new home. Although he was told of new families, good ones weren't awaiting for him. He stayed four years before they even indentured him. But, as he grew older, his luck ran out — for he found no love. Physical abuse — locked in sheds without food — abandoned — left on Sundays to work while they attended Church.

Shifted from home to home, they couldn't find a family to love my grandfather. He was returned to New York. Now, you have to understand, he could speak French...but he couldn't speak English. So his life became worse. I often wonder why he held on. Back in a new land — can't speak the language — rejected twice over.

(In) 1916 he was sent back to Louisiana....Rumor has he was still abused here, seems his life got no better. Francis finally made a good home...worked on a farm along with a brown hair girl...(in 1923), 20 years old, with all his life ahead — past behind, he married this girl.

As his family grew, Francis never cared to discuss his life. (He cried of the neglect.) He used to say, 'They didn't want me then, I don't want them now.'"

Marguerite Thompson

Source: Marguerite Thompson, from Johnson and Hall, *ibid.*, pp. 224-227.

"The Larsons had two sons other than Teddy....My new Papa...was a big man with a moustache and a kind face. The Larsons were of the upper class in that area. They had a lady that came and washed the clothes on a wash board. Another lady made all of our clothes except for our underwear. Mrs. Larson (Mama) would make all of our underwear.

My new home was a big two story house with 10 rooms, but we didn't have any electricity. The house was beautiful inside....I didn't have a bedroom of my own. I slept on the couch in the frontroom on a feather mattress Mama would take out of her closet every night. After a few weeks, she said I could do it myself. The boys had bedrooms upstairs. Teddy and I were not permitted to use the bathroom. We had to use the outside toilet, and on Saturday we would drag a galvanized bathtub from the back porch and put it by the cook stove.

Mama didn't like my New York accent at all. She wanted me to talk like they did, so I was slapped quite often in the mouth. Sometimes I would wonder what I had done wrong.

I had only been there a few weeks when Teddy brought out a china doll to play with. He said it was his and I couldn't play with it. Well one day I found it and took it outside and broke it. I got my first whipping....

They rented out three of the bedrooms to salesmen. When I was six, Teddy and I started school. When we came home from school we had to wash the dinner dishes from noon. Then we had to go upstairs and make the beds, dust mop the floors and clean the bathroom. We didn't dare use the toilet, she said it took too much water. By the time we got through with that, it was time to set the table for supper. I always only had one helping put on my plate. Teddy and Charles always had milk to drink with their dinner, but she said I couldn't have any.

They had two cows and a lot of milk and Teddy and I would deliver it both morning and night. Charles [age 14] went with us a few times until we could do it on our own. Sometimes I went by myself, especially if it was cold. One morning on my way to school, it was so cold that the sidewalks were very icy and I slipped and fell. One bucket of milk hit the sidewalk, the lid blew off, and half of the milk spilled out. Well, I got up, put the lid back on, and set it on the porch where it was supposed to go. The lady called my foster mother and wanted to know why she didn't get a full quart of milk....When I went home at noon (my foster mother) told me about it and wanted to know if I drank some of it. I told her what had happened and she said I was lying. Then she got the rawhide whip and didn't even care where she hit me.

Between the ages of six and eleven I got many whippings....I can truthfully say I never got enough to eat. When I would come home from school and go to the pantry to get a piece of bread and butter, she said I was stealing it, because I didn't ask for it.

...Once a year a Mr. McPhealy would come from the (N)ew York Foundling Home to see how I was getting along. I had to tell him fine. I would have to speak a piece for him, or poetry as it is called now. The name of it was 'Looking on the bright side.' Then I had to dance the Irish jig for him and when I was through I was excused. I would go outside and cry and wish he would take me back with him. I wanted to tell him the truth about how I was treated, but I couldn't. Still, she would whip me if she thought I was lying, which I was lying to Mr. McPhealy....I often wondered why Papa Larson didn't ever have anything to say about the way she treated me, but it seemed to me like she ruled the house."

Alice Blanche (Bullis) Ayler

Source: Alice Blanche Bullis Ayler, from Johnson and Hall, *ibid.*, pp. 442-443.

"[My brother] Elmer was 'adopted' by a deaf-mute couple. He was kept in the bath tub during his waking hours. This was their method of caring for him. [When Elmer was three], the couple had their 'own child' and gave Elmer back to [the society]. He heard adults discussing him, and the fact that he 'wasn't right' because he had not learned to talk — and never mentioning the fact that he had never been talked to. This, and the rejection of a second time by people, affected his image of himself throughout his life time....A rural home for me was found outside of Marion, Kansas. The hard work of 'hand pumping' the windmill, for the cattle tank, proved too much for the little girl that I was. I was then 'put' in another farm home in Marion, Kansas.

I received great psychological ridicule here, and was constantly threatened to be 'sent back to the home.' I stuck it out and worked part-time for J. C. Penney, while attending high-school. At seventeen years, I was placed on my own by the social worker, as she considered me to be responsible and able to care for myself."

Unknown artist's rendering of a young girl at work in the kitchen.

Alice Ayler's story has a happy ending, as do most of those told in recent orphan train story collections. She raised a son and a daughter (the latter adopted in her determination to prove "that you could love a child, not of your 'own blood.'") Alice started college at the age of fifty and earned a master's degree in counseling psychology. She later reflected:

"In retrospect, I have had a good life, in spite of the early heartaches. Asked if I resent being removed from my home, I answer, 'no — it was the best thing that could have happened.' My bad environment was altered so that I could use the native ability I was born with. It has always been a challenge to me to prove I could do something that people thought I couldn't do, because of my parents. The responsibility for their life, is not on my shoulders.

As a footnote to this story, my mother eventually took my sister back to care for. Even more interesting, is the fact that she 'took' a handicapped child, later in life, and cared for her. This, after having given 'five cute little kids' like us away, causes a little bitterness now. This bitterness wasn't there previous to learning about this."

How the Orphans Fared

Some of the orphans fared well indeed. They became members of loving families, were well-educated and treated with every kindness. Others were not so lucky; chosen for their value as workers, some were treated no better than slaves, beaten and overworked. Below is a transcription of the indenture contract of a baby girl, who was placed with a couple from the state of New Jersey. This editor has no further record of how the child was treated, but the reader is not to assume that the relationship between Ida Goudy and the Shafers was an unpleasant one.

The words underlined in the text indicate those which were handwritten on the printed indenture form. A few words were ineligible, and are so indicated. (Courtesy of the Orphan Train Heritage Society)

The Indenture of Ida Goudy

In Indenture, made the <u>thirty first</u> day of <u>March</u> in the year of our Lord one thousand eight hundred and <u>seventy one</u> between THE AMERICAN FEMALE GUARDIAN SOCIETY, of the first part, and <u>Rick and Alice Shafer, Columbia, County of Warren, state of New Jersey</u> of the second part. *Whereas,*

<u>Ida Goudy</u>

a <u>fe</u>male child, who was of the age of <u>one year</u> on the <u>twenty fifth day of June</u> last, has been duly surrendered by the natural, or other legal guardians, to the care and management of the said Society; and *whereas* the said <u>Rick and Alice Shafer</u> has applied to the managers of the said Society to put out and place the said child with them by adoption, and as an apprentice, until such child shall arrive at the age of <u>twenty one</u> years. *Now this Indenture witnesseth,* That the parties of the first part, acting by their Board of Managers, and in pursuance and by authority of an Act of the Legislature of the State of New York, entitled, "An Act to incorporate the American Female Society, passed the 6th day of April, 1849," and with the approbation of <u>the commissioner of the [illegible] of the city and county</u> of New York, have put, placed and bound out, and by these presents do put, place, and bind out, the said

<u>Ida Goudy</u>

as an *apprentice*, unto the party of the second part, to dwell with and serve them from the day of the date of these presents, until the said apprentice shall attain the full age of <u>eighteen</u> years. During all which time the said apprentice shall serve, on all lawful business, according to her power, wit, and ability, and shall honestly, orderly, and obediently in all things, demean and behave herself towards her said employer, and all others. And the party of the second part, for <u>themselves, their</u> executors and administrators, doth covenant and agree, to and with the parties of the first part, and their successors, that the party of the second part, during all the term aforesaid, shall and will provide and allow, unto the said apprentice, competent and sufficient meat, drink, and apparel, washing, lodging, mending, and all other things necessary and fit for an apprentice; and shall and will teach and instruct, or cause the said apprentice to be taught and instructed to read and write, and so much of arithmetic, spelling, and grammar, as is needful for persons in the ordinary ranks of life; and shall also give unto the said apprentice, at the expiration of the said term of service, a new Bible and the <u>sum of one hundred dollars ($100)</u> in money, or a satisfactory equivalent, and shall cause such apprentice to attend public worship on Sunday, and the Sunday-school, (whenever such attendance is not too inconvenient,) during all the term aforesaid, and frequently to read the Holy Scriptures aloud; and shall not allow the said apprentice to be absent from the service of her said Employers without express leave; nor suffer her to haunt ale-houses, taverns, or play-houses; nor to play at cards, dice, or any unlawful game; but will exert their authority to cause and procure the said apprentice to behave herself in all things, as a faithful apprentice ought to do, during the term aforesaid.

Although the present instrument binds the above-named child, strictly as an apprentice, it is nevertheless, the true intention of the parties of the first part to place, and of the party of the second part to receive, said apprentice as an adopted child, to reside in the family of the party of the second part, and to be maintained, clothed, educated, and treated, as far as practicable, with like care and kindness as if she were in fact the child of the party of the second part.

And it is further agreed, by and between the parties to these presents, that if the said apprentice, or the Indenturing Committee, shall, at any time within three months from the date of this Indenture become dissatisfied with her situation or employment, or if the party of the second part shall, at any time within that period, become dissatisfied with the said apprentice, that then, and in either such case, it shall be the duty of the party of the second part to give notice of such dissatisfaction, either on their part, or on the part of the said apprentice, and forthwith to return the said apprentice to the parties of the first part, and thereupon this Indenture shall cease and become void to all intents and purposes; and further, that girls over the age of ten years, when thus returned, shall be entitled to two dollars per month, or an equivalent in suitable clothing, such wages or clothing to be accounted for to the Indenturing Committee. But after the expiration of three months from the present date, without any such notice of dissatisfaction from the party of the second part, or the said apprentice, or said Indenturing Committee, then this Indenture is to be and continue in full force. And it is further understood that information, verbal or written, respecting the welfare of said apprentice, will be required at least once a year, and that a specimen of her handwriting, in letter form or otherwise, must be transmitted from time to time. And it is further provided, that the present Indenture shall not be construed to render the said Society responsible in damages for any cause whatever, but shall only operate as the full exercise of the powers conferred by its charter for the purpose herein expressed.

IN WITNESS WHEREOF, the parties of the first part have caused their common seal to be affixed to one copy of the present Indenture, and the same to be also attested by their Children's Secretary. And the party of the second part hath, at the same time, set their hand and seal to the other copy thereof.

Present
John J. Van Kirk

Richard B. Shafer
Alice M. Shafer

I approve the preceding indenture:
[Two illegible signatures]

Still, despite rumors around the country that the New York organizations were "deporting trouble" to the midlands, few of the orphans were reported to fall afoul of the law. Virtually all, according to later reports, grew up to be fine citizens and raised loving families of their own.

Source: 1917 Children's Aid Society report, from Fry, *op. cit.,* p. 79.

"...the roster went like this: A Governor of a State, a Governor of a Territory, two members of Congress, two District Attorneys, two Sheriffs, two Mayors, a Justice of the Supreme Court, four Judges, two college professors, a cashier of an insurance company, twenty-four clergymen, even high school Principals, two School Superintendents, an Auditor-General of a state, nine members of State Legislatures, two artists, a Senate Clerk, six railroad officials, eighteen journalists, thirty-four bankers, nineteen physicians, thirty-five lawyers, twelve postmasters, three contractors, ninety-seven teachers, four civil engineers, and any number of business and professional men, clerks, mechanics, farmers and their wives, and others who have acquired property and filled positions of honor and trust. Nor would the roll call be complete without mention of four army officers and 7000 soldiers and sailors in their country's service [during the World War I era]."

John Green Brady

"(John Green) Brady had fled his home in New York when he was seven. His mother was dead; his father, a long-shoreman who drank, beat him whether he was drunk or sober. The police finally picked the boy up and deposited him in the city orphanage. One of those who had been in Noblesville [Indiana] on the day [in 1859] the train pulled in with the 27 waifs from Randall's Island was Judge John Green of Tipton. 'It was the most motley crowd of youngsters I ever did see,' the judge was fond of telling in later years. 'I decided to take John Brady home with me because I considered him the homeliest, toughest, most unpromising boy in the whole lot. I had a curious desire to see what could be made of such a specimen of humanity.' Judge Green lived to see Brady [who became a trader and missionary] graduate from Yale and Union Theological Seminary; the judge's widow saw her foster son become a three-term Alaska governor."

Henry Segar

Source: Reginald Segar, writing of his father, from Johnson and Hall, *op. cit.*, pp. 147-148.

"No one ever came to inquire about Henry [Segar, at the New York Foundling Home], so in April 1907 [at age 3 1/2] he was placed on an Orphan Train and sent to Opelousas, Louisiana.

He was initially taken in by a Lavergne family who had one daughter and lived with their parents in Lawtell, Louisiana. An early eye-witness related to me how curious everyone was the day Henry arrived. He was considered different and was the subject of many pranks and jokes. His first foster father died and his foster mother remarried a man who physically abused Henry.

My aunt (my Mother's sister) remembers how Henry would come to school and was very very quiet, a loner, couldn't seem to learn anything and would have belt marks showing in his body. She related how she felt so sorry for him. He only made it to the 3rd grade. He was also forced to work hard in the fields as well as around his house. He himself would not talk much about his early life and most of my information had to come from people who knew him at that time. When Henry was about 16 years old, he left this horrible environment and was taken in by Mr. Theo Dejean who had a grocery story in Lawtell. [*Henry became a good businessman and Mr. Dejean's widow gave him the store and some acreage in thanks for help he had given her when her husband died young. He married and had a son.*] Henry never seemed to have just

53

one job; he grabbed every opportunity that presented itself. He sold fertilizer, was a railroad agent, an insurance salesman with two companies, an elected Justice of the Peace, and involved in politics. He was a Justice of the Peace for 21 years and then chose to give this up to run for and be elected to the St. Landry Parish School Board where he served for 18 years until his death in 1974 at age 70."

Some orphans made no attempt to discover the truth about their original families, while others conducted a considerable search. Often, records were scattered or destroyed, however, some train riders were eventually reunited with their families.

Peg Kildare

Source: Peg Kildare, from Johnson and Hall, *ibid.*, pp. 355-356.

"To begin with, I think I'm one of the lucky 'Train Riders.' I was wanted, loved and spoiled by the people who adopted me. I really don't remember anything about the train ride, nor do I remember being in the New York Foundling Hospital.

My mother, Marie Buckman, placed me in the home when I was only three weeks old. Records show that she never came back to see me, nor made any inquiries about me. This has always been a sore spot in my life, as I do think she could have at least inquired as to how I was....I did not try to get any information about my background until both my adoptive parents were deceased. Mother never wanted me to discuss it. I learned that I was adopted accidently, when I was eight or ten years of age. The census taker came to the house doing the school census. When mother found out what the census taker wanted, she told me to leave, but, being an inquisitive child, I crawled under the porch and listened to what they were talking about. Was I ever surprised when Mother told her I was born in New York. That really was a shock to me...threw me for a loop. I waited several days and then asked Mother if she had ever been in New York. When she said she hadn't, I said, 'How come I was born there.' Then she had to tell me she'd adopted me. I really went into 'orbit.' I cried, wanted to run away, hated my mother, etc. I finally calmed down, but it took several days. Mother kept saying, 'She didn't want you, but we did.'"

The End of the Line

The placing out of orphans and unwanted children from New York and other eastern cities continued until 1929, when the last orphan train rolled into Missouri. Ironically, at the dawn of the Great Depression, times had changed; newer social philosophies and agencies believed it was better to keep the original family together and worked toward that end. The farms were changing, too; machinery mechanized agriculture so that fewer farmhands were required to work the land. The government became more involved in social issues as the modern system of welfare was introduced. The swell of immigrants dwindled, and child labor laws diminished the appeal of the orphans as "free" workers.

The experiment had been a success in many ways: thousands of children found happy homes (although countless others suffered cruelty or indifference along the way). The crime rate in New York City dropped significantly during the period of placing out. Compulsory education and slum clearance in the cities reduced the number of street waifs. The end came for one of the largest emigration movements of children of all time.

Then, with the trains stilled, the orphans were often forgotten as well. Perhaps as a result of the renewed interest in history and genealogy fostered by the American Bicentennial celebration in 1976, folks began to look into their past. Among them were some of the last of the remaining orphan train riders, most of whom had long since died. Societies like the Orphan Train Heritage Society of America sprang up in the Midwest to gather the stories of the riders and their descendants before they were lost to the prairie winds. The result has been several collections of orphan train riders' memories, all well worth the effort required to find them and read them from cover to cover.

Parallels between the Orphan Train Experience and the Adoption Experience

Source: B. J. Allender Douglass, from "The Orphan Trains of 1853 - 1930 and Their Effect on the Development of Adoption Policies and Practices," *Social Work Perspectives*, Volume 5 Number 1, Spring 1995, San Francisco State University, San Francisco, California, pp. 39 and 41-42.

...Although the orphan trains stopped running in 1930, the adoption policies of the times remained, many of which are still used today. Alarmingly similar are the stories of the orphan train "riders" and adoptees of today. Secrecy of records, anonymous pasts, lost identities and shame are among the most crucial of issues that are shared between the two groups.

The placing out programs of 1853-1930 did serve a purpose: many children and adults were in fact offered a better life in the country living and working on farms. However, careful examination of the experiences of the orphan train riders suggests a parallel to the experiences of adoptees that can shed light on current adoption policies and practices, and offer insight as to how we can upgrade the quality of life for adoptees and other "orphans" and their families (Bellingham, 1984). Specifically, it seems clear that social workers need to look at the usefulness of the sealed records law, study how the adoption process affects the self-esteem and healthy identity development of adoptees, and examine how our society as a whole treats orphans and adoptees differently from other children — and how we might go about changing that....

Bill Oser

Source: Bill Oser, from Johnson and Hall, *op. cit.*, p. 387.

"... I guess we orphan kids are a special breed of individuals. As orphans we asked for just the basic things in life, along with someone to guide us, so when the time came to go out into the world we had a chance to survive and eventually made it. We asked for little, and when the hour approached to start the race through life, the record shows, there was no stopping us and no limit to our dreams of success. President Kennedy once said to his fellow country men, 'Ask not what your country can do for you, but what you can do for your country.' I would not be surprised if some former orphan whispered that quote in the President's ear."

An artist's rendering of new members of a Western family.
(Harper's New Monthly Magazine, *August 1873*)

Bibliography

Bellingham, B. W. (1984), *'Little wanderers': A socio-historical study of the nineteenth century origins of child fostering and adoption reform, based on early records of the New York Children's Aid Society.* Ph.D. dissertation, University of Pennsylvania.

Dolberger, Judith A., editor. *"Mother Donit fore the Best" Correspondence of a Nineteenth-Century Orphan Asylum.* New York: Syracuse University Press, 1996.

Fry, Annette Riley. "The Children's Migration." *American Heritage,* vol. 26 #1, December 1974, pp. 4-10.

Jackson, Donald Dale. "It took trains to put street kids on the right track out of the slums." *Smithsonian,* vol. 17, August 1986, pp. 94+.

Johnson, Mary Ellen and Kay B. Hall, eds. *Orphan Train Riders: Their Own Stories.* Baltimore: Gateway Press. Published for the Orphan Train Heritage Society of America. Vol. 1, 1992.

"The Little Laborers of New York City." *Harper's New Monthly Magazine,* vol. 47 #279, August 1873, pp. 321-332.

Riis, Jacob A. *How the Other Half Lives; Studies Among the Tenements of New York* (1890) Republished: Cambridge, MA: Belknap Press of Harvard University Press, edited by Sam Bass Warner Jr., 1970.

Tears on Paper: The History and Life Stories of the Orphan Train Riders. Compiled by Patricia J. Young and Frances E. Marks. Bella Vista, Arkansas; self-published, 1990.

Wheeler, Leslie "The Orphan Trains." *American History Illustrated,* vol. 18 (December 1983), pp. 10-23.

Further Reading

Bunting, Eve. *Train to Somewhere.* New York: Clarion, 1996.
Picture book for read-alouds or very young readers, telling one girl's touching story. Fiction.

Fry, Annette R. *The Orphan Trains.* New York: New Discovery Books, 1994.
History for middle readers.

Holt, Marilyn I. *The Orphan Trains: Placing Out in America.* Lincoln, Nebraska: University of Nebraska Press, 1992.
A scholarly examination of the orphan trains for older students and adults.

Nixon, Joan Lowery. *The Orphan Train Quartet:*
A Family Apart (Bantam 1987).
Caught in the Act (Bantam 1988).
In the Face of Danger (Bantam 1988).
A Place to Belong (Bantam 1989).

Warren, Andrea. *Orphan Train Rider: One Boy's True Story.* Boston: Houghton Mifflin, 1996.
The story of Lee Nailing alternates with the history of the orphan trains. Elementary school reading level.

For more information on the orphan trains, contact:

Orphan Train Heritage Society of America, Inc.
P. O. Box 496, Johnson, AR 72741-0496

About the Editor

Jeanne Munn Bracken is a librarian and a writer. Living in the Boston area for the past twenty-eight years has sparked her interest in history. Her fascination for genuine historical characters was fostered as a seasonal guide at the Ralph Waldo Emerson House in Concord, Massachusetts. She is a reference librarian, a long-time columnist for the Littleton (Massachusetts) *Independent*, and has written numerous articles and commentaries that have been published in newspapers and magazines from coast to coast. Her books include *Children with Cancer* (Oxford University Press, 1986) and *It All Began With an Apple* (history of the Veryfine Products juice company, 1988 and 1994 editions). She also edited, for the Perspectives on History Series, *The Shot Heard 'Round the World: The Beginnings of the American Revolution; Iron Horses Across America: The Transcontinental Railroad;* and *Life in the American Colonies: Daily Lifestyles of the Early Settlers*, with several others in preparation. Jeanne lives in Littleton, Massachusetts, with two daughters, three cats, a rabbit, and her husband Ray, who was adopted as a toddler and is anticipating a reunion with his original brothers and sister.